THE LITTLE BOAT
and other
Short Stories of GOD'S GRACE

Fran Rogers

THE LITTLE BOAT
and other
Short Stories of God's Grace
1st Edtion

© 2016 Fran Rogers
Father and Family Books

ISBN-13:978-0692680476
ISBN-10:0692680470

fatherandfamily.com
godsgracegodsglory.com

Cover by Danielle Camorlinga
Photography by Nando Pereira

Dedicated to our son, Andrew
who has helped us see that with goals and focus
visions can become realities.

Contents

About the Author

Rubber Legs

S tan, a young man in the prime of his youth, successful in all that he had wanted to do in life, woke one morning, but was unable to get out of bed. His legs and arms were like rubber.

He could move his head, his hands, his feet, and his body, but his arms and legs seemed to have no bone, and no muscle. He was not in pain---but totally uncoordinated.

Overnight he had become helpless.

Alone, he had no one to call to. He could not reach his phone. His screams for "help!" went unanswered. In his despair he cried, "Oh God, help me!"

In the assurance that his cry was heard he ceased to panic, and his struggle turned to resignation. He gave in to his helplessness with the only hope he had been given. In peace, he relaxed and slept. When he awoke, Stan realized that the trauma he had experienced had been a dream.

Was it only a dream? Or was it God's supernatural way of revealing his real need, and producing a miracle in his life? It was real enough to cause this young man to evaluate his independence of God. In the dream he had experienced in his whole being the sense of full dependence on the Lord God, who had enabled him to call out to the only one who could help him in his solitude, and the response he received was what he needed.

In reality he sought the same God of mercy that he had encountered in his dream. God brought him to full dependence. And he never forgot his rubber legs and arms.

God restored, through his relationship with His Son, Jesus, the proper use of his whole body, soul, and spirit. In a local church body of believers, Stan learned more about his God, and found his true purpose for living, in service to Him, for His glory.

Even the youths shall faint and be weary,
and the young men shall utterly fall:
But they that wait upon the Lord
shall renew their strength;
they shall mount up with wings as eagles;
they shall run, and not be weary;
and they shall walk, and not faint.
Isaiah 40:30-31

THE OLD MAN

The *old man* was as mean as they come, living by his own standards and not caring for people, except what he could get out of them. He had built a financial empire after his wife died—he didn't really miss her because she was always a hindrance to his own self-fulfillment. He was morally unsound, set in his ways, and totally unprepared for the change that was to come. His daughter and her husband, killed in an automobile accident, left their tiny baby in his care.

He had not even participated in the care of his own daughter, so he was at a loss, as to how to take care of this *child*. But, he agreed to accept the responsibility. He was given a special book of instruction, and found help, support, and fellowship with a local group of parents.

Feeding and changing the baby was not so difficult, and he slept most of the time, but the older the *child* became, the more the old man had to read the instruction book. The *child,* as he was growing up, was taking more of his time. This *child* knew what was in the instruction book and telling him what they were supposed to do.

The *child* was changing the *old man.* In circumstances that he would normally have gone his own way, the *child* was a reminder that it was not the right way for either of them, so he conformed to the way of the *child.*

He began to notice many changes in his life and his acts of *goodness*; he had a sense of *humility*, instead of pride; *kindness* where there had always been contention; *generosity* in place of greed; *compassion* where there had always been apathy or contempt for his fellowman.

Where he used to have the mind of an *old man* he had become young in heart and spirit, living a life of love for God and his neighbor, in fellowship with others, like the *child* to whom he had given his life.

He had *put off the old man* and *put on the new man.* He was *"in Christ, a new creature. The old had passed away; the new had begun."* (2 Corinthians 5:17)

The *new birth* gave him *a new spirit* and *a new heart* that beat a different way, in rhythm with its creator. (John 3:3; Ezekiel 36:26; Colossians 1:14-16))

"So then it is not of him that willeth, nor of him that runneth,
but of God that sheweth mercy."
Romans 9:16

We do not produce this *new birth*, but in God's timing, He gives the *new heart* and *new* life. At first it may seem easy, and then, it becomes more difficult for the *old man* of Adam, to give in to the child of God, because more is demanded. This child speaks to our hearts, to convict and guide us from our own way, to *the old paths, wherein is the good way---*God's way.

Guided by God's Word and His Spirit within us, we live the *eternal life* of God through death to self. The old life to self-will and independence is overwhelmed and overcome by a divine love that brings us into fellowship with God, the Father, His Son and His Spirit. Though it is a personal experience it is shared with those of His family, and one of *unspeakable joy*. (1 Peter 1:8)

We praise the Father for loving us, for redeeming a people for Himself, showing mercy and compassion on miserable sinners, changing hearts, giving new life, and making us His own forever.

Seeing that ye have put off the old man
with his deeds;
And have put on the new man,
which is renewed in knowledge
after the image of him that created him;
Put on therefore, as the elect of God,
holy and beloved,
bowels of mercies, kindness, humbleness of mind,
meekness, longsuffering;
Forbearing one another, and forgiving one another,
If any man have a quarrel against any;
even as Christ forgave you, so also do ye.
And above all these things put on charity,
which is the bond of perfectness.
And let the peace of God rule in your hearts,
to the which also ye are called in one body;
And be ye thankful.
Colossians 3:9-16

3

Apprehended

On the "Most-Wanted" list of criminals was a man named Sinner. He became known as the worst of his family. He was from a long line of Sinners, some of which the authorities had arrested. Most of them were crafty enough to elude the police, went into hiding, and finally died.

But this one who had broken almost all the laws on the books became the central point of the officers' work in the county where he lived. He was wrecking havoc on the whole community, and was becoming a hero especially among the young people. He became so well known and admired that the people named the town after him. After all his descendants had helped found it.

The whole area was becoming a Sinnertown---idolatries, witchcraft, hatred, jealousies, wrath, strife, murders, and drunkenness was the way of life. Some of the local authorities who could not control all this, just joined them. Sinnertown became a popular place. People began moving there from everywhere so they could be free to practice their own lifestyle.

Finally, the federal government had to step in. From the highest authority in the country came a man named Grace. He set up his office in the local church, and stayed in the home of friend who lived in Sinnertown.

At first, it seemed that he was not doing anything. The few people who had called the federal authorities for help kept waiting and wondering what he was doing there---and why he had even come.

He kept a steady path between the church and his friend's home. After a while he brought others into his confidence. Still there was no visible evidence of his doing anything about the Most-Wanted criminal in Sinnertown.

In the meantime, everyone became curious, thinking, "He is making no effort to find this man."

Then, one day he announced a meeting in the church. All were invited. But what did they do when they got there, but sing and pray and talk about somebody called The Lord God, who had a Son, named Jesus.

This went on each week for a while, and gradually one by one, the people were turned.

Not all, but some saw the folly of their lives, in light of the life that Grace showed them.

A freshness came over the community. Some scoffed, but they did not stop what Grace started, and because Sinner had been receiving news of everything that was going on in Sinnertown, he became curious. He wanted to meet this man called Grace, but he knew he would have to come out of hiding.

Others of his own family came to him, those who had met and come to love Grace. They told him that being of the notorious Sinner family, and living in hiding the rest of his life was no life at all. He saw how happy they were, a joy he had never seen in his family before.

And so, Sinner was drawn from his little world. The day he walked into town, face to face with Grace, he knelt in front of him, held up both hands, and said, "Take me, please, take me. I am Sinner, have mercy on me."

At that moment you could have heard a glorious sound of the angels in heaven.

Sinner was tried, convicted, and pardoned that very day as he confessed all that he had done. A crowd of witnesses who promised to love him, care for him, teach him, and walk with him, surrounded him. They all promised each other the love and care that Grace had taught them.

The name of the town was changed again, to Graceville. It grew, and more of the Sinner family was drawn, and apprehended, arrested by the Spirit of Grace. *The law of the Spirit of the life of Christ* that *delivered them from the law of sin and death* was established in their hearts. They were given a special book from which Grace had taught them, so they did not forget, and believing the promise that one day they would see this man, Jesus, to be with Him, forever, they grew *in the grace and the knowledge* that comes from Him, understanding that Jesus had sent Grace to give them this *new heart* and life in preparation for His coming. They would wait for Him, love Him, praise Him, love each other, and tell others about Him. They would be the means of God's grace to apprehend others.

I sought the Lord, and afterward I knew
He moved my soul to seek Him, seeking me.
It was not I that found, O Savior true,
No, I was found by Thee.

"Not as though I had already attained, either were already perfect, but I follow after, if that I may apprehend that for which also I am apprehended of Christ Jesus. "
Philippians 3:12

The heavenly Father who **bought** us *with the blood of the everlasting covenant of His Son, our Savior* [Hebrews 13:20] who **sought** us by His Spirit of Grace; who **brought** us to Himself; keeps us in His grace, draws us closer to Him, giving us this desire to *follow after* and take hold of all that we know of Him—to His Glory and our joy.

4

HEAVEN IN A BUCKET

The Lord said to me, "At the end of each day bring me all your thoughts from that day in a bucket. This will be your test of how much you have of heaven."

I found a small bucket, but before the end of the first day I needed more than one. Little did I realize how many thoughts one mind could have in a single day.

With three small buckets I approached God's throne.

He sifted through my buckets, asking where I had gotten each thought.

In reply I answered, "That one from a book; that one from a magazine; that one from a friend." Others I tried to remember, but didn't know how they got there.

"There's not much here of heaven ~ a few words of prayer for a friend, but not much else." He said.

As I returned home and prepared for bed, I wondered why there were no more thoughts of heaven in my buckets that day. As I settled in bed to sleep, I decided that I would do better, and have some thoughts the next day that would please God.

I found a larger bucket the next morning and set about to collect what I thought God wanted.

Looking in the library I came across the writings of the great philosophers.   As I diligently searched through these I could see the Lord's pleasure; my bucket was filling up. I felt so good about my new thoughts and myself. Then, I went to talk to a friend ~ who had a brilliant mind and a PHD in science and physics. Before the day was over my bucket was almost full.

Let's see ~ what else can I put in my bucket? There's an excellent movie playing at the local theater ~ one destined for an academy award.   And it was a wonderful movie. My bucket was full.

Well, how did I do today, Lord."

"You have really been busy," He said, as He examined the contents, "But I find nothing here of heaven, not even a prayer."

"If this isn't part of heaven, what is all this that I thought was so good." I asked.

"It's all of the world, dear." I'll see you again, tomorrow."

That night before bed I knelt and acknowledged that I didn't know what He wanted, but I would try harder tomorrow.

The first thought the next morning was that, perhaps the bucket itself was all wrong. Maybe it attracts the wrong thoughts. So I set out to find the best and biggest bucket I could find for that day's thoughts.

I found the perfect one ~ advertised as the one "that you need for your best thoughts" ~ quite expensive, too, but knowing that this would be what God was looking for, it was worth the price.

But that day dragged on without success. And becoming depressed about what I should have in my bucket, it began to fill up with tears. It was almost too heavy as I carried it ~ and it became heavier as I continued crying.

The way seemed longer that day, but the closer I came the lighter the bucket seemed.

As I reached God's throne of grace He smiled, and said, "Seems that you have sprung a leak in that expensive bucket."

"Why can you smile, Lord, when I feel so terrible ~ and look~ after I searched all day my bucket is empty?"

"I can smile, my child, because you have finally discovered the secret. No bucket in the world will attract and contain the things of heaven. As the creator and ruler of my kingdom, I have determined the kind of receptacle you need, and the thoughts that will fill it."

As I bowed before Him I asked for this vessel and His knowledge of heavenly things. I submitted, as He said I must, my bucket and all my human efforts of pleasing Him.

He gave me a "new heart and a new spirit" that only "seeks His kingdom and His righteousness," and makes me continually aware of His spreading His love of Jesus in and through me.

Through His Word and prayer, m*orning by morning He wakens my ear to hear as those who are taught.* Isaiah 50:4

"By His mercies" each morning "I present myself" to Him to be "filled with His fullness" all day ~ no longer "conformed to this world, but being transformed by the renewing of my mind. His thoughts are kept and "obeyed" in my heart and life as He keeps me by His own power.

His kingdom is *coming* and *His will is* being *done*, in me, *as it is in heaven.*

"And the God of peace .... make you perfect in all things....working in you that which is pleasing in His sight through Jesus Christ, to whom be glory forever. Amen." Hebrews 13:20-21

5

THE BANK

The young widow, with her three small children and baby, was on the streets again. Since their father died the children had enjoyed getting out of their small basement apartment during the pleasant autumn weather. They had been meeting and talking to people, and receiving handouts. It was no different now, though the days had become cold and blustery. They knew that there would be no food on the table if they stayed at home.

Sarah was not out with her children begging people for food and money, but had been asking the people that she met, "Could you tell me where to find The Bank?"

Most often they would ask, "What bank? Lady, there are many banks in town."

Her reply was always, "I don't know what bank. All I know about is The Bank."

"There is a bank two blocks down on the left," said one man she talked to.

She and the children walked the two blocks, entered, and talked to the woman at the front desk. "My husband told me before he died that he had been putting money each week into the bank. My children and I need the money for food and rent. Do you know if this is the bank where he was putting his money?"

The receptionist called the manager who came out of his office, and asked her, "What is your name?"

"Sarah Grady," she replied.

"And what was your husband's name?" the manager asked.

She said, "His name was John Grady."

Checking their accounts he told her that they had no account in that name.

As she turned to leave, the manager asked if she had any proof; any papers that her husband had left to show what bank he may have used. She knew of none, and could not remember him ever mentioning the name of the bank.

She was always so busy with the children that she had little time for anything else, except to prepare food, wash clothes, and clean. Her husband did all the shopping, always remembering to bring her a pack of cigarettes. She had begun smoking when she was sixteen and this was the only pleasure she got out of life except caring for her husband and children. He would not buy her cigarettes when she was pregnant, but as soon as she had a baby he would bring her a pack. Now, when anybody offered them money the first thing she would buy was a pack of cigarettes. She could make them last a long time; one would get her through the day.

The same scenario occurred every day, with the same results. No bank within walking distance of their apartment had an account in the name of John Grady. She made the mistake of telling one young man why she was looking for the bank. He took them to lunch in a local restaurant. There he quizzed her, hoping that in helping her find the bank she would reward him by sharing the money with him. He could not help her find the right bank, and so he, like many others, left them to find their next meal elsewhere.

Others, though not going out of their way, gave them money, or bought them groceries. Some directed them to The Food Bank, and the shelter for the homeless.

The cold days turned into snowy days, and it seemed as if Sarah and the children would just have to give up their daily excursions, stay inside, and hope for the best. But the children believed that they had to continue their search for The Bank, and did not want to give up, no matter what the weather might be. With determination they wanted to venture further than they had gone before, to continue to look for and hopefully, find The Bank. And so they planned to start out on a Sunday afternoon, to walk as far as they could; rest, and begin again the next morning.

They talked to no one. Most whom they saw already knew what they were looking for, and just shook their heads. Sarah and the children walked as far as they could, until their hands and feet were almost freezing. The baby needed to nurse, the children were hungry, and sleepy, and Sarah was exhausted. "Just a little further until we find a place to stop and rest for the night," she thought. Finally, in the distance they saw lights from a small church where the members were having their evening worship service.

"We can stop for a while," she told the children. "We will have to go in quietly, so no one will know that we are here." Inside they saw a door that led to the basement area, where they slipped downstairs, deciding to hide there until the morning. They were so tired, and the warmth of the building so comforting that, as soon as they were still, they all slept, except Sarah. As she nursed Annie, she could hear the Psalms and hymns being sung upstairs. "Surely God must be in this place," she thought to herself. She had never heard such heavenly sounds.

As the music stopped Sarah and the baby drifted into a sound sleep.

Upstairs in the sanctuary the pastor began his message for the Lord's Day evening from the text of Matthew 25:31-46; his emphasis, "You gave me meat; ye gave me drink; ye took me in; ye clothed me, ye visited me, ye came unto me.---When?---Inasmuch as ye have done it unto one of the least of these my brethren, ye have done it unto me."

The message ended, and the last hymn sung, the congregation adjourned to the fellowship hall downstairs where food and drink were waiting. When the lights were turned on, Sarah and the children were not affected, for they were still sleeping, but the people were astonished, surrounded Sarah and the children. and fell to their knees. As if to acknowledge that the Lord was there and had brought them *the hungry, the thirsty, strangers, and those in need of clothing*, they began to praise the Lord for His goodness, and to pray for them.

The hearts of the people at Christ's Church were moved, and committed to take in this widow and her children, and to care for them.

With the excitement, the children were awakened, one by one, to see the table of food, to the joyful faces of the people, the hugs and the welcome. Thinking that they had found The Bank, they woke Sarah, who was not only surprised, but thought that she must be part of a dream. Someone held the baby while someone else helped Sarah fill her plate. While they ate she told the pastor who they were, where they had come from, and why they were there. An older couple offered to take them home to stay the night, and to talk the next morning about how to find The Bank. Sarah still thought that she must be dreaming.

Pure religion and undefiled before God and the Father is this, To visit the fatherless and widows in their affliction, and to keep himself unspotted from the world. James 1:27

Mr. Harris, an elder in Christ's Church, and Mrs. Harris, were gracious and merciful to Sarah and the children. He led them in family worship before they went to bed, reading the 23rd Psalm, and afterward they sang the Psalm together. Sarah thought, "God must be here, too."

As she lay in bed that night she wished that *the Lord*, which Mr. Harris spoke of, could be her shepherd and the shepherd of her children. What would it be like to have God as her Father, and to know the protection and provisions that He gives? Had He not been taking care of them all these years? And as a child had she not, though from a poor family, had all that she needed? Many questions were on her heart as she finally settled down and slept with her children near her.

At breakfast the next morning, and before every meal, Mr. Harris would ask God's blessings for the food. After the meals, he would lead them in family worship.

Their whole life was focused on God, the Father, His Son Jesus Christ, and the Holy Spirit.   He prayed for wisdom, grace, and guidance for Sarah and the children, and asked how the church could help them.

A blizzard began that night so they had to wait until the weekend before they could go back to their apartment to get their things. They would stay with the Harrises while looking for The Bank. Sarah had time to tell them of John and her moving east from Arkansas when she was pregnant with Johnny.   His uncle offered him a job as a plumber's apprentice. The uncle had died before John had finished his training, so the business dwindled, except for odd jobs. Then John was injured in a motorcycle accident and died a few weeks later. Though her parents offered to take them back to Arkansas with them, Sarah insisted on staying until she found The Bank.

When Mr. and Mrs. Harris drove her to the small, furnished apartment there was a *For Rent* sign in the yard, empty trash cans were at the curb, and the lock had been changed. Looking through the window Sarah saw nothing of their own things. Mr. and Mrs. Harris hugged her. She cried, and said, "We didn't have much, but all that we had is gone."

Mrs. Harris, understanding the situation, in deep sympathy said, "The owners must have thought that you were not coming back. We'll help you start over. Everything will be new for you from now on."

"When I find The Bank I'll pay you back for everything," Sarah replied.

"We'll contact the owner and have your mail forwarded," said Mr. Harris as they drove away.

On the way back to the Harrises Sarah
was very quiet. Her heart was greatly moved
as she thought about all that she had
experienced during that week. There had
been calls from the pastor, elders, deacons
and families of the church asking about Sarah
and her children. They planned to meet that
night to discuss how they would help them.

Back at the Harris home, Sarah asked to
talk to them about Jesus. She began humbly,
"You have made me feel as if we are part of
your own family. We have never seen or
heard anything such as we have this week. As
we have been a part of your daily worship we
have seen and heard how the Lord is your
shepherd, in mercy providing not only for
your needs, but also for the needs of others. I
want the Lord Jesus Christ to be my shepherd
and the shepherd of my children. I want God,
His Father, to be our Father, too. I want the
guidance of the Holy Spirit like He guides you
and His church."

"Sarah," Mr. Harris said, "Do you understand why you need a shepherd?"

"Yes Sir," she answered. "We are all sinners, not knowing that we are lost sheep. When Jesus speaks to our hearts by His Holy Spirit, He wants us to come to Him, so that He can keep us from sin and take care of us forever."

"Can you do this by yourself?" Mr. Harris asked."

I don't think so," said Sarah. "I have heard you pray and thank God for His mercy and grace, and for drawing His people to Christ. Is it not a supernatural thing that the Father brings people to Christ by His own Spirit? Do we not have to agree to His covenant of grace, giving ourselves to Him, just as He gave Himself for His sheep? He has made it easy for me to come to Him. We have nothing except the clothes we wore here and what you have given us.

I have not had a cigarette since last Saturday and have not wanted one since I have been here.

Right now all I want is what you people have in Christ---the Savior, the Lord, the Shepherd, the Father, and His Spirit."

Mr. Harris then asked Sarah, "Are you willing to give up looking for The Bank?"

"Do you think that I should? How will I repay you, and how will I know what I should or shouldn't do the rest of my life?" she replied.

"First," He said, "Let us go to Him. If, by His goodness He has given you *a new heart and a new spirit*, you can pray in the name of Jesus. Talk to Him as you would to a Father; tell Him your heart's desire, and repent of your sins. Praise Him for His grace and mercy to forgive your sins; thank Him for being your Savior and Lord, and ask Him as your heavenly Father, to guide you by His Spirit, and to care for you and your children.

He knows your heart and will accept you into His covenant as you offer yourself to Him."

Such a sincere, spirit-filled prayer of repentance and faith the Harrises heard, and were blessed to witness a new birth into the Father's kingdom. Sarah was regenerated, and converted to become a child of God that day. (1 John 3:1) She was soon after baptized into the body of Christ's Church.

In the days that followed, Sarah and the children served the Harrises, willingly, as gratitude became their second nature. She learned from Mrs. Harris how to cook food they had never eaten before, how to sew, how to care for a home, and her children, and by Mrs. Harris' example, of how a wife should love her husband, and live in submission to him.

With the church's help Sarah tried, unsuccessfully, to locate The Bank. Finally she gave up the idea as she invested more and more of her life in Christ, caring for her family, the needs of the church and anything the Lord put in her heart. The Shepherd of her soul met all her needs. (1 Peter 2:25)

A few years later Sarah married a young widower who had two small children, and they had three of their own. They continued in daily family devotions to the Father and their Lord Jesus Christ who had brought them together. They taught their children the Psalms and hymns that Sarah had heard that first night, and had come to love. As they were shepherded they brought up their *children in the nurture and admonition of the Lord*. (Ephesians 6:4) They taught them to be aware of the people around them, to think of others before themselves. (Philippians 2:3) Christ's Church grew as they continued to minister in His name.

We can only guess why John Grady's bank account was never located. (We could have put a twist on the story and had the money turn up later, or had Sarah receive a big insurance check.) He could have drawn the money out without telling Sarah. He could have used a bank in another town, or opened the account in another name. It doesn't really matter. However there are some things we can learn from this story.

One thing we can see is what the spirit of hope can do in a person's life. What if John had never told his wife about a savings account? She would have had nothing to look forward to except an occasional cigarette. Her husband was gone but she did not become despondent. She had something to keep her going. She believed what her husband had told her, and acting on faith she had a purpose and persevered.

If we truly believe what God tells us we will persevere through our trials and difficulties. We will see His sovereignty and providence at work in our lives and the lives of others.

Her hope was instilled in her children. Even when she might have given up, the children still believed, and hoping that they would find what they thought to be true, they wanted to continue until they reached their determined end. A humble child-like faith is an encouragement to others.

If you say that false hope is deception, we would respond by saying that God, by His sovereign grace, can turn false hope into true faith. Believing that He, in His providence uses all circumstances to bring His people to Himself, we can see how God plans, how He puts things together, and reveals Himself, His Son, His mercy, His grace and His provisions. In the process of looking for The Bank Sarah found something better, something eternal--- the real savings account was found in Christ, deposited in His Church.

The true church---Christ's Church--- wherever it is located, will be a ministry in the name of Christ to the lost and needy. It will be a model of Christ and His mercy. It will reveal God as a heavenly Father who cares for His children. It will preach and strive to practice the instructions of His Word. It will be a unit, described in the New Testament as one body with many members, whose desire is to discern the heart of God, the mind of Christ, and the working of the Holy Spirit in all of life.

All coming as sinners in need of God's mercy and forgiveness, the whole body of believers---all ages---lives for the Father's glory, with the desire to *grow in the grace and knowledge of our Lord Jesus Christ.* (2 Peter 3:18) Where do we find such a church today?

Much of charity is a seasonal thing for today's church. Christ's church is a ministry year-round. There are people, single and with families, all around us who need the

Shepherd. I pray that God, our Father, will use us to look for them, and to be ready to minister to them when He brings them to us. We have been where they are, and the Father was merciful to us. I pray for His Spirit to *shed abroad His love in our hearts*, that we may *love Him with all our heart, soul, mind and strength, and our neighbor* (wherever we find them) *as our self*---for His glory and our joy.

Wherefore putting away lying,
speak every man truth with his neighbour;
for we are members one of another.
Let him that stole steal no more:
but rather let him labour,
working with his hands the thing
which is good,
That he may have to give to him that needeth.
And be ye kind one to another, tenderhearted,
forgiving one another,
even as God for Christ's sake hath forgiven you.
Ephesians 4: 25, 28, 32

6

THE TENT

In a small town, a revival was planned. In anticipation of the many that would come, a tent was erected. No building would hold all the people. This revival would be one based solidly on God's word, and not so much on the preliminaries. Where God's word had become secondary in the churches His plans were to bring the people back to it, that they might know Him.

After months of prayer for God to do His work in those who would come, the night of the first service began with the lifting of voices in praise to Him.   Those who came with humble hearts, and eagerness to hear God's word, sat close to the front, so as not to miss any of the message they wanted to hear.

As the preacher began to speak, all listened attentively, until suddenly a noise from a storm outside distracted most of them.   Though the message continued without interruption, a few, and then most of the congregation, moved from their seats to find their way outside to their cars. As the lightning and thunder did not cease, neither did the word that was being preached.

Some were undecided, whether to leave or to stay. They were torn between the evidence of what was going on outside and what they were hearing inside.

"Fear not, it is I, do not be afraid."

"Let not your hearts be troubled."

"Lo, I am with you, always."

"In this world you will have tribulation, but be of good cheer. I have overcome the world."

"Perfect love casts out fear."

Many were overcome by past fears, even the experience of fierce storms that had devastated many lives, and they only trusted their own means of action --- to move and find better shelter.

In the course of the storm those who left the tent were either overcome in the deluge, or sat in their cars to wait until the storm was over.

Those who remained in the tent were so caught up in the word of God that they were not aware of the raging tempest outside. Then, their subsequent praising and rejoicing silenced any confusion and noise going on around them.

When the service ended, they walked out to see and to minister to the brokenness and the pain outside --- to prove the truth of the words they had heard spoken. Their faith spoke love to those who could not yet believe.

There is a supernatural realm of God's glory that provides a covering of grace for those who accept His word as the only means of life, apart from all that we already know and have experienced.

When Jesus said, "The kingdom of God is at hand," He meant, "In me and my words are the revelation of something not of this world." He had come --- sent from God, the Father "from whom every family in heaven and in earth receive its true name," to bring the word of God to the people. He was and is, "the way" --- the revelation of God, and the only means of our repentance and salvation.

If we give up our own way of thinking, and as Paul states in Romans 12:1-2, "present our bodies to Him," we can be "transformed by the renewing of our minds;" and thereby prove in this form He created, "His good, acceptable and perfect will."

His word has the power to do this. As any information accepted, read, and taken as truth will conform us to what it says, so the Divine word of God is "light" and "power" to make those who are adherent "holders" of it in their thinking and in their hearts the reflection of it.

By His word then we become what He created us to be --- a living, visible image of the living, invisible God of glory, love and grace.

We who are recreated (regenerated, redeemed in Christ) and living by its power in us, meet Him as sentinels in the morning watch (together as the body of Christ wherever we are) walk into each day as soldiers of His word, "with the praise of the Lord on our lips and the two-edged sword in our hands." (Psalm 149)

We minister to the wounded of the world and bring them to the word of God where they too have the inner strength, to believe, and to be a reflection of His word, His glory, His love, His grace.

Such is the seed of Life, to be received in the fertile heart, to grow, to produce the fruit and more seed of the Divine Life, of the Father.

Such is the sweet fellowship of the Father and Son, through the knowledge of His word in Christ; all working by the power of His Holy Spirit.

7

THE LITTLE BOAT

The following story is a result of God's working in three particular areas ~ ~ in my own study and prayer; in my praying for wisdom to write a letter to encourage our granddaughter, Kourtney, who was turning eighteen, and graduating from high school, and in my memorizing, playing and singing the hymn, O the Deep, Deep Love of Jesus.

Michael was a young man who, as a child, heard, read about, and saw movies of distant places. It became his heart's desire to see the world. So, getting an education, then a job, he saved his money. Forgoing marriage until he realized his dream, he made his plans, and one day booked his passage on the largest cruise ship that he could find.

Having come to the day of fulfilling his dream, he arrived with his luggage at the port of departure. The gigantic ship *Pride* was appropriately named. Even from a distance its size and presence took his breath away. There was this huge world within a world, beckoning him to enter, to come away, and enjoy his success. How proud he was to see his plans coming to fruition. The ramp into the ship was ample for the multitude that was boarding upward into his dream.

Awe-struck, he practically tripped over himself as he carried his stuff to the ship. As he struggled toward the ship, a man standing by asked if he needed help.

He said, "No, I can handle it."

At the same time a small sign next to the man caught his eye.

It read, "Boat to Paradise."

"You have a boat?" Michael asked.

"Sure," the man answered, pointing to the end of the dock.

Michael said, "I don't see it."

"Would you like to?" the man asked.

He replied, "Sure, I have a few minutes before my ship leaves."

Walking to the end of the dock he saw this small fishing boat with a set of oars. Snickering to himself, Michael said "So, you take people to Paradise in your little boat?"

Understanding Michael's cynicism the man answered, "Yes, I do, one at a time."

Now that his curiosity was stirred Michael asked, "How many people have you taken to Paradise?"

The man answered, "Only a few; not many people believe me, and so miss out on this one; most prefer the big ship, and all the other places."

Michael's interest, more than he could control, questioned once more, "How much do you charge for your little excursion?"

The man replied, "There is no money in exchange; just understanding that you have to leave your baggage here. You don't need to take anything with you; everything you will need is provided for you. You must also be willing to follow instructions. You must listen to my directions. I must teach you how to get through the rough waters; how to survive the long, slow passage, and prepare you for your arrival. Without this dependence on me you will not make it, nor would you appreciate what you experience when you get there."

Michael had one more question as he looked out over the ocean. He saw beyond the cruise ship the brightness of the sun, but in the direction of the small boat there were clouds. "Do the cruise ships dock at Paradise?"

In reply the man said, " The cruise ships are too big. The inlet is only large enough for this small boat."

Michael by then was intently drawn to this man; somehow he believed that what he was offering was true. The man was not forceful. He was not arrogant. He was meek in his manner, yet very strong.

Michael, out of the corner of his eye, saw the cruise ship *Pride* move away from the port, as he, with the help of the man's hand, stepped down into his little boat. As the man moved the oars across the waves, rippled by *Pride,* the little boat became steady. Michael watched as his dream ship got smaller and smaller. Further out he saw the ship sink into the horizon.

Far out in the ocean, beyond sight of land, they passed through rough waters. They experienced rain, thunder and lightning, yet without fear or harm. After the settling of the storm, Michael and the man talked about life. They compared the differences in each of theirs. Michael learned much that he had not been taught in the schools he had attended. The man told him that Paradise was a place owned by his father, who sent him to invite and accompany those whom he wanted to share his huge estate. Each one there had been given a portion of his kingdom, and had the means and the liberty to go and come, as they desired. Some brought others back with them to receive the same blessings.

Even before they arrived at their destination Michael's dream had changed. He believed that there was a place, a Paradise, prepared, and revealed to only a few. He learned that humility was the only means of getting there. Reaching this destination meant trusting the one who was bringing him there.

Not everybody will need an explanation of this parable, but for those who might ~~ Michael represents those who trust in, and follow Christ, with whom God planned to save His people. His Son knows the way of humility. Having been born in humble surroundings of poor parents, brought up as a carpenter's son, Jesus, the Son of God and Man, lived humbly, and so died humbly, by the pride and hands of men. By His mercy He saves us from the sin of pride and destruction; by His grace He gives us a portion of His kingdom, and brings us to live with Him eternally.

Only He can teach us, and lead us in the way of humility. There is no way to God except in Him, and the power of His Spirit working in us, to loose us from pride; that we may see it for what it is, to loathe it; to love and cling to the Savior. It means total dependence on Him; not on ourselves, on others, or the things of this world.

In the reality of Christ, our fantasies fade away. True joy in this world is living in light of the promises of that eternal paradise with

Him; each day humbly waiting on Him, as He works His will in us and prepares us for His glory.

Humility is accepting all things as they come; believing in His sovereignty and plans for us, praising Him in all things as we *seek His kingdom and righteousness*, anticipating that He will lead us to know Him and what He desires for us. One on one with Christ is sometimes a lonely life, away from the business and frills of the world, but this alone is true life and happiness. In His plans for us He brings us together with others who are following Him.

8

The Broken Cup

She sat on a table ~ a $.25 item at Mrs. Palmer's garage sale. After being packed away in the attic for so long, Littlecup was glad to breathe the fresh air and to be in the company of people again. Years ago she had been a frequent guest at Mrs. Palmer's tea parties, held and filled with sweet tea.

"Here's a nice lady," said Littlecup. "I hope she needs a cup." "No?"

"Well, maybe this gentleman ~ "Oh!! Careful !!!" He was no gentleman!"

For hours Littlecup waited, hoping that she would not be taken back to the attic.

The next day a young couple came, looking for furniture.   Finding none, they turned to leave, when the young lady spotted Littlecup, "Don"t you have enough teacups?" Eddie said.

Holding the cup so tenderly, Ginger exclaimed, "This one is so special."

"You said the same thing about all the others," said Eddie.

"But this one reminds me of the set of teacups Mom had.   She and I had the neatest tea parties when I was a little girl," replied Ginger, as she placed a quarter into Mrs. Palmer's hand.

With both hands, Ginger held Littlecup until they arrived home where she placed her on a shelf.   Littlecup was surprised to find herself among many others.   There were at least 20 other cups --- different shapes, colors, and sizes.

"Well, at least I'm in the open, and free to look around ~ even if no one holds me or drinks from me again. She was beginning to feel good about herself when a teacup in the back of the shelf said, "Aren't you the dainty one.   I suppose you think you're special because Ginger and Eddie brought you home."

"Well, no," said LItttlecup, "But I'd rather be here than stuck away in an old box with the spiders and silverfish."

As the spokeman for the collection, Bigcup informed her of how things worked in the Bradford household.

He said, "Ginger uses her newest cup when she has her friends for tea."

The next week Littlecup was shown off to Ginger's friends as Ginger served tea in her special teacups. Littlecup was the last cup Ginger purchased, and for many weeks the main one that Ginger used when she made tea.

Littlecup became proud of being No. 1 Teacup. Some others felt jealous, discouraged, and rejected.

Going to the shelf one day Ginger said, "Now which of you shall I fill with my new blend of tea?"

One cup said, "Me!"

Another said, "No, me!"

Bigcup pushed from the back, saying, "It's my turn, I'm tired of sitting on this shelf everyday."

In the excitement Littlecup was brushed aside, and toppled over the edge. With tears streaming down her face, Ginger started picking up the pieces from the floor, saying, "I didn't want this to happen, Littlecup. When I started collecting my special cups I knew one might someday get broken. I could have used the others and given you a rest. But I knew that you needed to be held, and to be close to me. The first time I picked you up and held you on the way home, you had a special place in my heart, just as the others I had found and brought home. The others would soon have their turn again, after you were feeling secure. Now you're broken, but we were prepared if this should happen. We have glue for my special cups. You'll need a while to set and heal. Soon you'll be like a new cup. And remember, though, that being special is no reason to boast. When you are healed you will sometimes have to sit on the shelf while I am using other cups."

As Ginger and Eddie set her in a quiet place to dry, Littlecup ~ feeling all warm inside, even without tea ~ thought to herself, "Just being a part of this collection and having a place in this family makes me special and secure."

About the Author

Fran Rogers is a wife/caregiver to her husband of 55 years, a 77-year-old great-grandmother, writer and blogger in Buford, Georgia. She writes from the experience of enduring many difficulties while living in the reality of God's grace. Through God's Word she has learned to be dependent on Him for all things, witnessing His love, joy, and goodness. Writing for over twenty-five years, she is now beginning to publish what God has been teaching her. The purpose of publishing is to share with God's people the legacy of His kingdom. She is a witness of God's provisions for all things of this life, and even more; the eternal life that He has prepared for all His people. The majority of proceeds from sales will be given to charity and to missions that witness of God's kingdom throughout this world. In view of Christ's promise that He would have witnesses in *Jerusalem, Judea, and Samaria, and to the uttermost part of the earth,* her hope is that God's people who read will not only benefit, but also promote this message to others through their purchase. Thank you for purchasing this book. Please consider leaving a review. Check the website fatherandfamily.com for more details of this ministry.

Other books are available, or soon to be published, in the series *Little Books About the Magnitude of God* and the series *What the Holy BIBLE Says*. Her work is longer than an article, but not as extensive as a regular length book.

Website: fatherandfamily.com
Blog: godsgracegodsglory.com
Facebook: Father and Family Books
Contact: contact@fatherandfamily.com